Dear Yoga, Thank You

A yoga themed coloring book for peaceful meditation.

Illustrated by Chelsea Radley

ISBN: 9781796295818

Imprint: Independently published

Published through Kindle Direct Publishing

Final approval May 2019

All Yoga quotes are credited when necessary

All artwork created on the Amaziograph app by Chelsea Radley and converted for ease of use in Adobe Illustrator by Chelsea Radley

Dear Friend,

Thank you so much for picking up this coloring book. Maybe you chose it yourself or someone gave it to you as a gift, either way, it has made it to your hands and my first thought is to thank you. As an artist, I have so many ideas floating around in my head and when one comes to fruition it is truly a moment of joy. So thank you for holding this completed work in your hands. It is an honor to know my art has made its way to you.

I don't know if you do you Yoga, or if you just enjoy mandala designs. Wherever you are at, you are here because something has drawn you to this point. In Yoga, you learn it's not about the poses themselves, pushing yourself into specific shapes, but as yoga teacher Adriene Mishler says, it's all about listening to your body, and "Finding what feels good." You can only do so much. So first forgive yourself for whatever is holding you back. Then accept what you can and cannot do, yet. I say yet because as I have persevered with my own yoga practice, I am learning there is much I can do that I did not think I could. The changes in my body are not outwardly noticeable, but they are making me stronger and healthier.

Much like yoga, the designs found inside this book were not achievable for me right off the bat. It's a common misconception that artists can draw anything. I have great respect for those that draw these designs by hand. They are meticulous and detailed. They require great patience. The skill required to achieve the desired result is built up over time. The very act of sitting to create can be its own form of meditation. And that is what all this artwork has been for me. It has been a way to quiet my mind, find peace in the way the lines form on my screen, and take that time needed for myself.

It's the same when you show up on your yoga mat. Just because you have a mat does not make you a fantastic yogi. Just because someone is flexible does not mean that they can immediately get to every yoga pose without injuring themselves. Yoga requires ease of movement and great patience. The muscles need to warm up and prepare to stretch. The toning in your body happens over time. And taking that time for yourself is so important.

My hope is that this coloring book helps you to relax, to meditate, to find peace. Be patient with it. Some of you may argue that you are not amazing at coloring and should not be trusted with a coloring book. Some of you are artists yourselves and my be critical of my own work yet desirous of the same peace that creating this brought me. Some of you have no clue what I am babbling about. Trust yourself. Laugh it off. And just enjoy the moment you are in. Find the peace when you can and know that the bit you find will help you throughout your day.

I love Adriene's saying, "Find what feels good." It's such a simple phrase and yet it is so poignant. It's not about the specific dos and don'ts. It's about showing up for that little bit of time you gift yourself, (make no mistake, it is a gift in this busy world), and simple enjoying the moment and what feels good about it. Take this book and try to just enjoy this moment of coloring, whether its inside the lines or not, and truly trust that it all starts at one point and grows from there. You can do this. I believe in you. Namaste.

~ *Chelsea*

What should you use to color this book?

Well, I have a few suggestions for you if you are new to the practice. Please take a look at these recommendations and understand they are only my opinion based on my own experience. The array of choices is thoughtfully suggested based on the quality of the tools themselves and the paper in this book. Different papers can handle different mediums. I have also tried to cover the array of low end to high end products. So without further ado, here are my suggestions.

Crayola products:

In general, I have found Crayola to be super reliable. They have a great line of products that are affordable and generally easy to start with. From their metallic pencils to their tri-tone True to Life pencils, to their watercolor palettes and even watercolor pencils, who among us hasn't started here? The great thing about Crayola is the affordable price for the product. You get to try your hand at a medium and see what you think before investing in the higher end products.

Walnut Hollow Oil Pencils:

These are a great product if you can find them. Walnut Hollow pencils aren't easy to find to my knowledge. The blending capability of these lovely pencils is top notch and the way they sharpen up to a nice point can't be beat for getting details. I personally have the set I do because my mother in law was cleaning out her closet and found them. I love them so much. Highly recommended.

Prismacolor Soft Core Colored Pencils:

Prismacolor is a highly recognized brand with lots of clout behind it. I have had some people tell me they don't like the soft core because they wear down so fast. They also are more delicate to sharpen because of the soft core. All that is true, but there is a reason the soft core is one I gravitate towards. It lays down lovely color and if you use the blending tools it is a joy to blend colors with. There is a variety of blending tools available for your use with these.

Fine Point Marker Pens:

There are three varieties I like for this category:

- Marvy LePen
- Stabilo Point 88
- Staedler Triplus Fineliners

All of these markers are hollow tip pens. This means they have a continuous flow but they also have a delicate tip. If you press too hard you will break these. They come in a variety of colors and even though some of them look alike they are all actually quite different. I have all the colors from all the different brands and I love them. The fine line is great for details and the variety of colors is great if you like options. Any one of these brands would be a great set to have. The advantages of one over the other aren't vastly different. They are all water based and hollow tipped. The only really difference is the type of grip you get. The Triplus is a triangular grip barrel. The others are rounded. Yes, there are other brands out there, but from what I have seen on the Amazon reviews I would stick with these three brands personally.

<u>Gelly Roll Gel Pens</u>:

By far the most expensive gel pens on the market but with good reason. They really are the best. I love the variety of color and texture you get with the different sets here. From sparkles to metallics to glaze to shadow. They have a lot of versatility and the colors are just gorgeous.

Let's take a quick minute to point out as well that if you prefer Amazon, that's awesome and that is mostly where I have found my supplies. However, check out JetPens.com for some really neat tools and tricks. They have most of these products and a lot of info on what to use and how to use it!

And there you have it in a nutshell (for an artist anyway because we can wax poetic on our favorite tools). The paper in most coloring books can't handed a heavier media and as long as you are careful with a water brush, using the water lightly and letting it dry between layers, using watercolor pencils shouldn't be a problem either. Crayola makes a nice set of these that are easy to use but Inktense is a more expensive highly saturated brand. You decide.

I hope this list will help you to further enjoy your own coloring practice. Enjoy and please feel free to tag me in your coloring posts. On Instagram @stxradley and #stxcoloring

May I live like the lotus, at home in muddy waters.

Namaste

Crown Chakra

I am connected to the divine source of the universe. I am light. I trust.

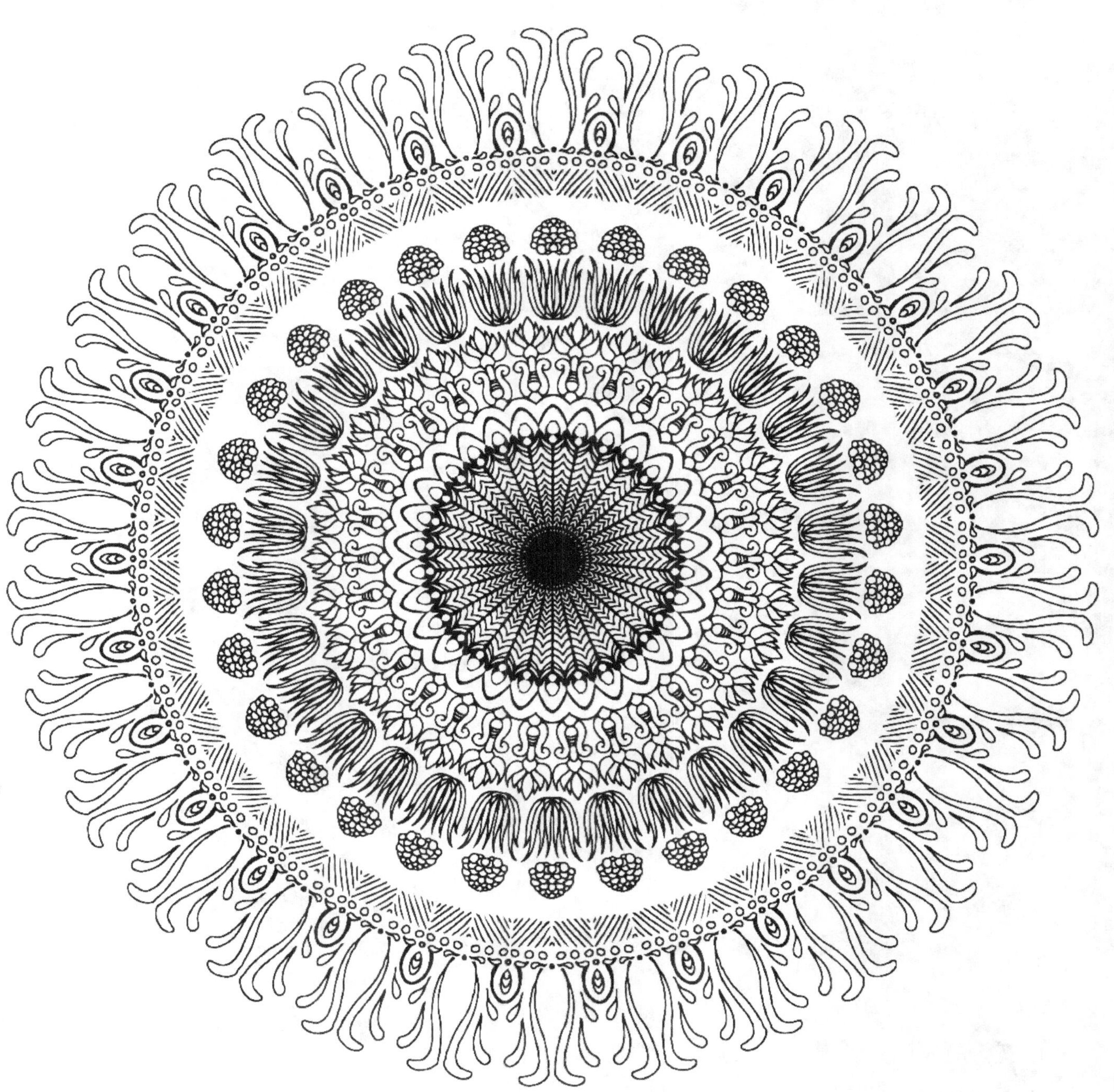

When you own your breath, nobody can steal your peace.

Third Eye Chakra

My mind is open to new vision.

I expand my awareness through my higher self.

Mountain Pose teaches us, literally, how to stand on our own two feet... teaching us to root ourselves into the earth...

_Carol Krucoff

Throat Chakra

I am alligned with my highest truth and communicate this with love and honor. My words echo softly within the universe.

My spiritual vision is clear. I always follow and honor my intuition. I see divine light in everybody. I look at love energy solutions from my higher self, before I choose love to react. I am spiritually awake.

Heart Chakra

My heart is open to receive the energy of love. I radiate this essence. I walk my path with ease and grace.

Do it with passion

or not at all.

Solar Plexus Chakra

My will and divine will are one.

I am cconnected to the abundant flow of the universe and manifest my dreams.

Be in
Balance

Sacral Chakra

I love all dimensions of myself.

I delight in weaving the creative tapestry that is my life.

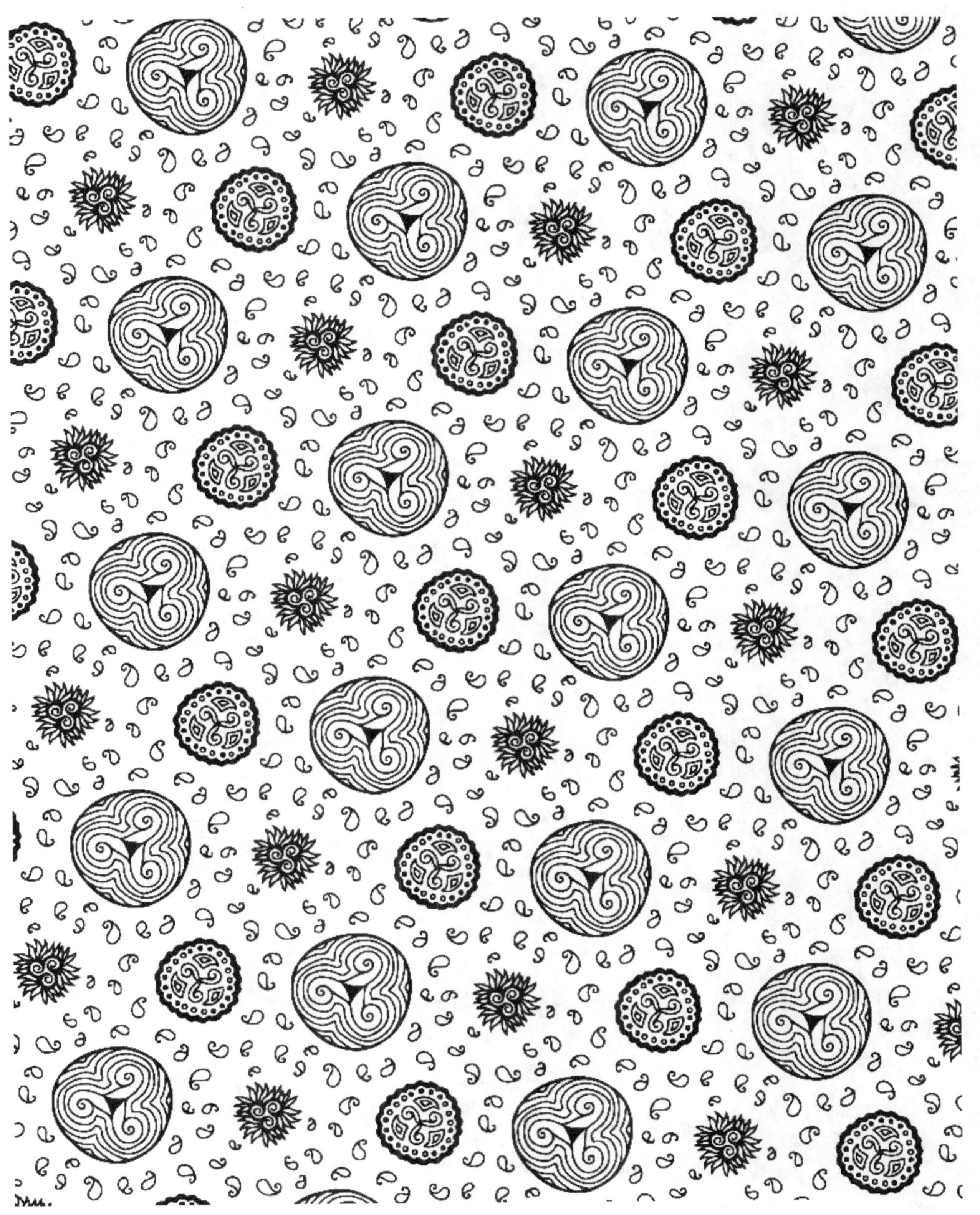

Root Chakra

I am connected with the energy of the earth. My body, mind and spirit are grounded, centered and purified.

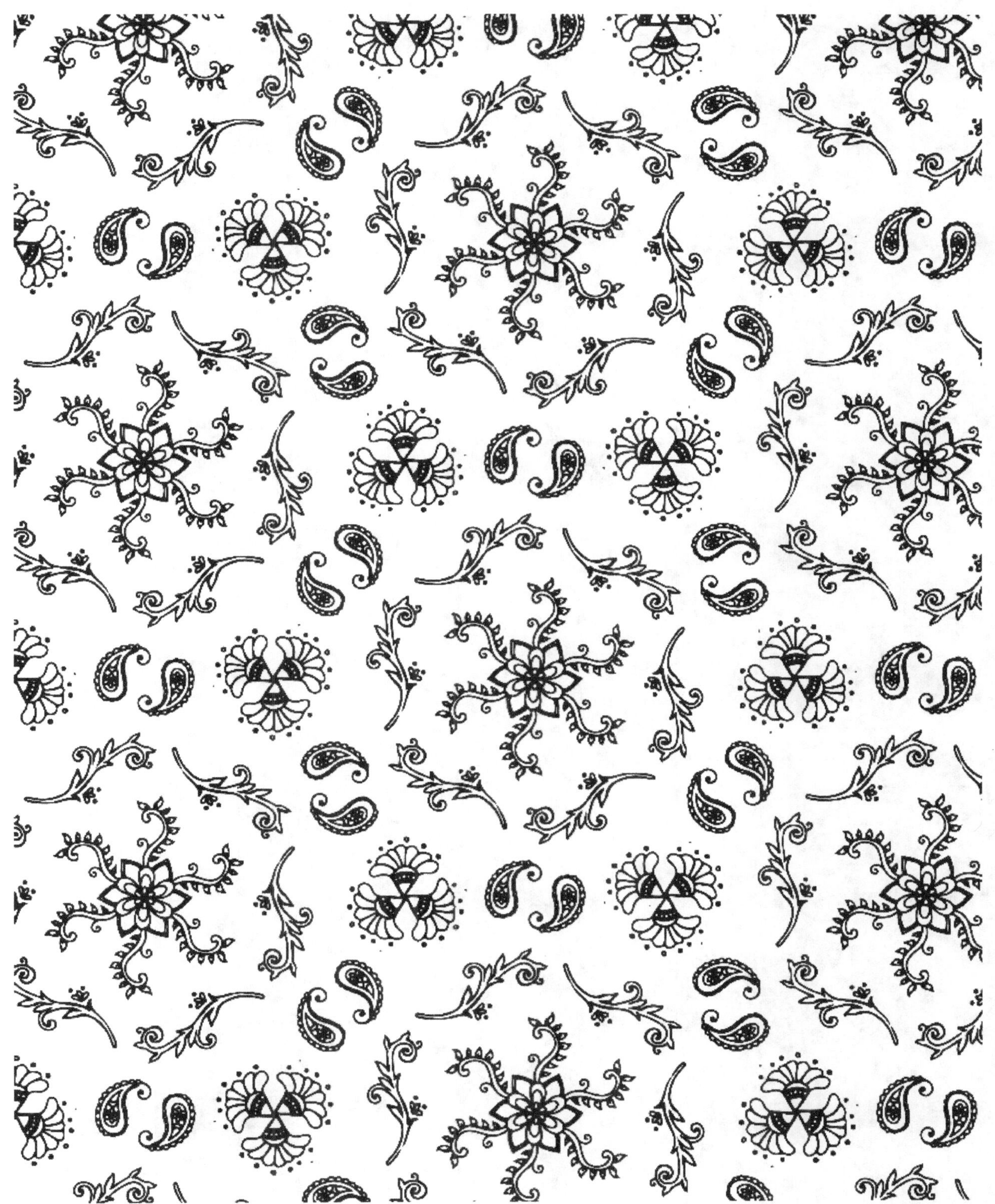

Be as the lotus: Open to the rising sun,

Unaffected by the muddy depths of its birth,

or even the water which sustains it.

Third Eye Chakra Mudra

I am calm and clear. I open to the wisdom that is within. I trust my intuition and follow it. I am connected to my higher self. I am the witness. I envision a world of peace and beauty. I release all attachments to wanting it my way. I see.

v

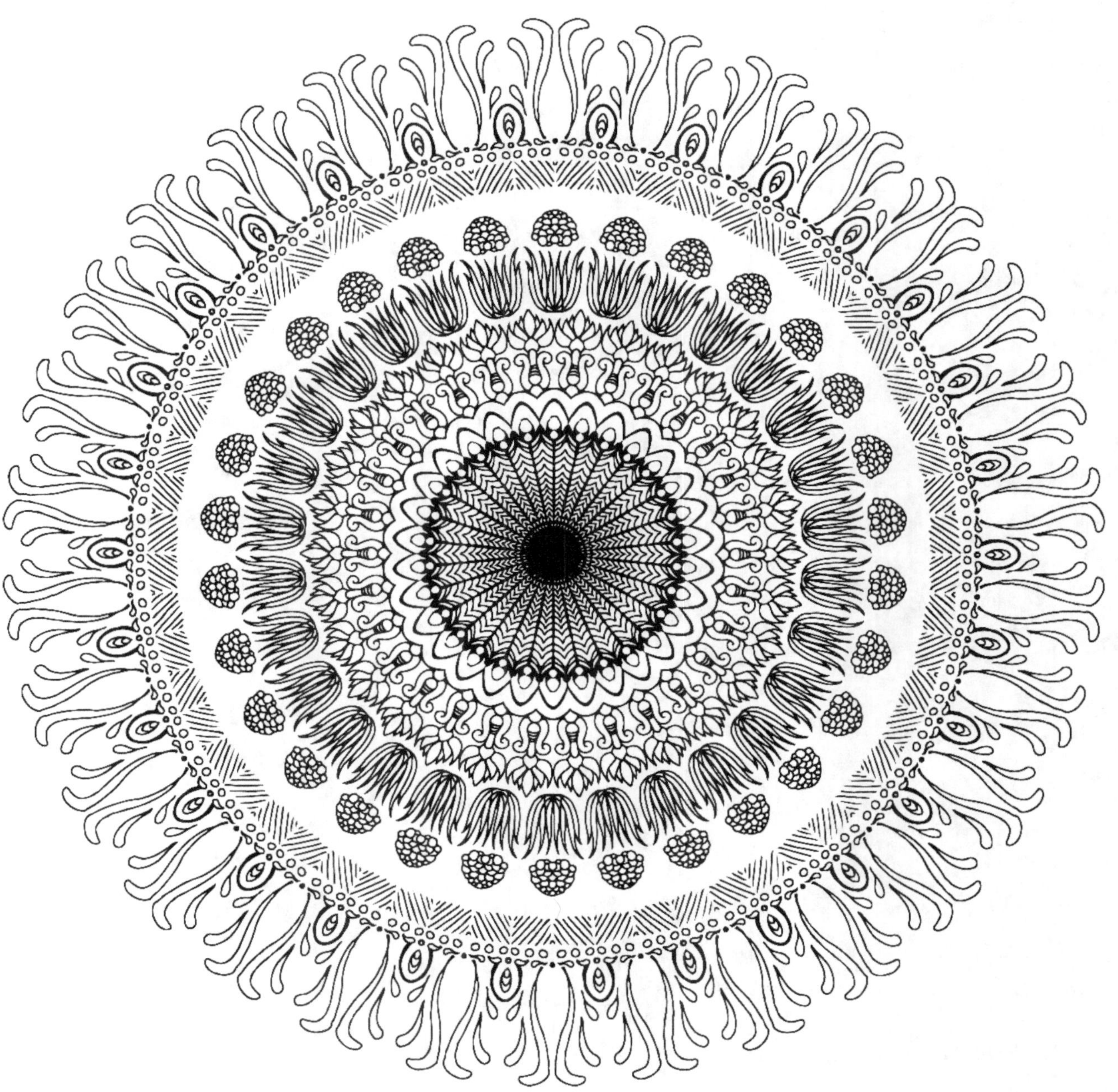

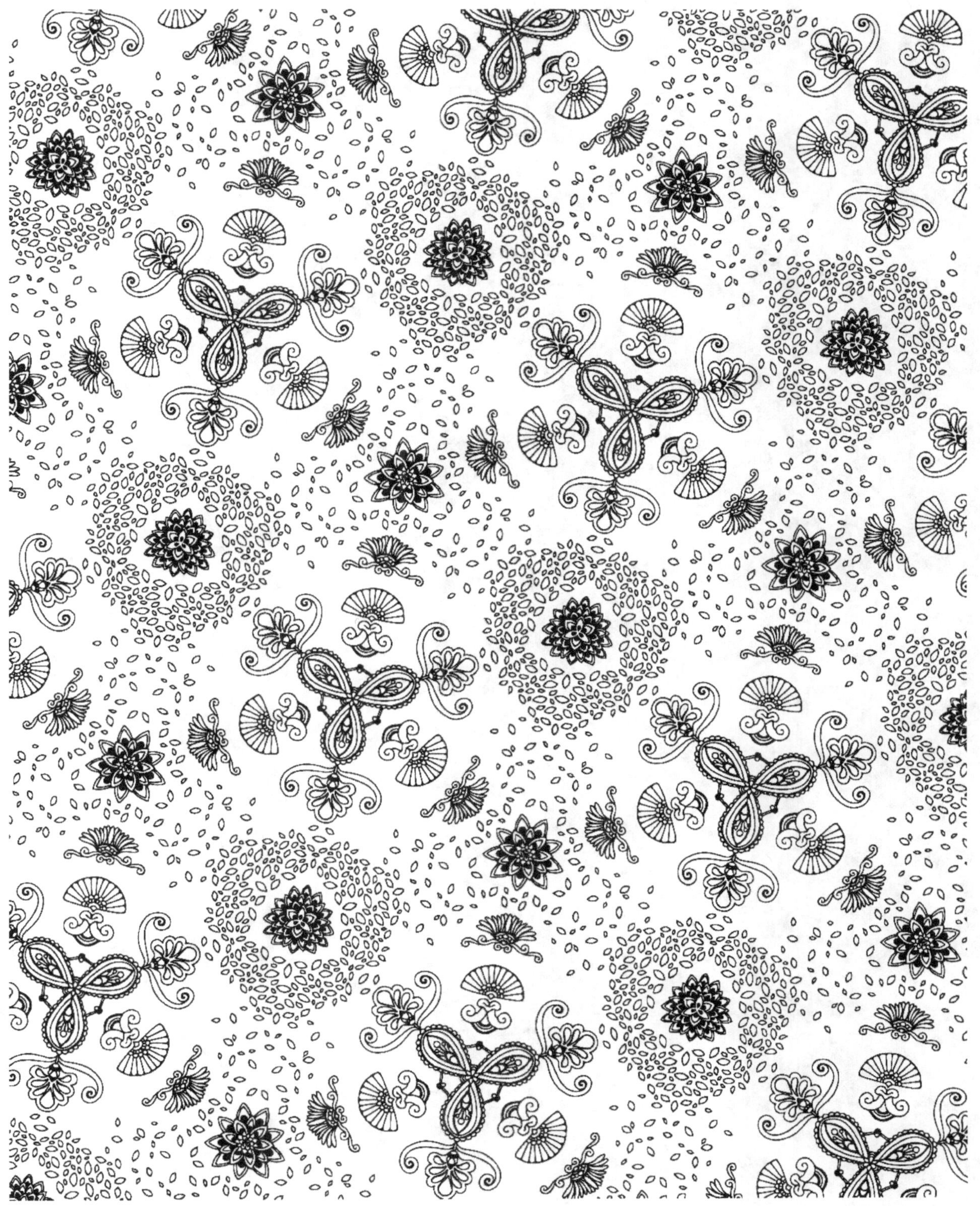

It's not your history, but your presence on the mat that matters.

Sri Krishna Pattabhi Jois

Crown Chakra

Third Eye Chakra

Throat Chakra

Herat Chakra

Solar Plexus Chakra

Sacral Chakra

Root Chakra

Namaste
The divine in me
honors the divine
in you.